Movement

with Gravity, Friction and Magnetism

Heather Rising

Movement with Gravity, Friction and Magnetism

Text: Heather Rising
Publishers: Tania Mazzeo and Eliza Webb
Series consultant: Amanda Sutera
   Hands on Heads Consulting
Editor: Jarrah Moore
Project editor: Annabel Smith
Designer: Leigh Ashforth
Project designer: Danielle Maccarone
Illustrations: Fabian Slongo
Permissions researcher: Liz McShane
Production controller: Renee Tome

Acknowledgements
We would like to thank the following for permission to reproduce copyright material:

Front cover: Shutterstock.com/Jose Angel Astor Rocha; pp. 1, 28: Getty Images/DigitalVision; pp. 3, 4 (bottom right): Shutterstock.com/Steve Byland; p. 4 (top): Shutterstock.com/revers, (bottom left): Shutterstock.com/Mckelehen; p. 5 (top): iStock.com/gorodenkoff, (bottom): Alamy Stock Photo/CBW; p. 6: Shutterstock.com/Rob Bayer; p. 7 (top): iStock.com/FatCamera, (bottom): Shutterstock.com/Pixel-Shot; p. 8: Getty Images/Martin Barraud; p. 9 (top): Alamy Stock Photo/Kuttig – Travel, (bottom left): Shutterstock.com/Sergey Ginak, (bottom right): Shutterstock.com/Just dance; p. 10 (top): Shutterstock.com/redknapper, (bottom): iStock.com/Karl-Friedrich Hohl; p. 11 (top): Alamy Stock Photo/Richard Watkins, (bottom): Shutterstock.com/Andrii A; p. 12 (left): Getty Images/Patrick Smith, (right): Alamy Stock Photo/Allstar Picture Library Ltd; p. 13 (left): Dreamstime.com/Dnaveh, (right): Alamy Stock Photo/DPPI Media; p. 14 (top): iStock.com/Guy Gross, (bottom): iStock.com/Jacob Wackerhausen; p. 15 (top): iStock.com/SimonSkafar, (middle): iStock.com/adamhodges, (bottom): Alamy Stock Photo/PA Images; p. 16 (top): Shutterstock.com/Benjamin Crone, (bottom): Shutterstock.com/Markus Mainka; p. 17 (bottom): Dreamstime.com/Matthias Wolf; p. 18 (top): Alamy Stock Photo/Panagiotis Kotsovolos, (bottom): Alamy Stock Photo/Gordon Scammell; p. 19: iStock.com/miles_around; p. 20: Alamy Stock Photo/The Canadian Press; p. 21 (top): Getty Images/Adam Pretty, (bottom): Alamy Stock Photo/Independent Photo Agency Srl; p. 22: iStock.com/JLBarranco; p. 23 (top): Shutterstock.com/Martin Valigursky, (bottom): Shutterstock.com/GregD; p. 24 (left): iStock.com/tylim; pp. 24 (right), 32, back cover (top): Shutterstock.com/TukkataMoji; p. 25: Shutterstock.com/Skycolors; p. 26: Alamy Stock Photo/World History Archive; p. 27: Alamy Stock Photo/NASA Photo; pp. 29 (top), 31: iStock.com/Fafarumba; pp. 29 (bottom), 30: iStock.com/andresr; back cover (bottom): iStock.com/Grafner.

Every effort has been made to trace and acknowledge copyright. However, if any infringement has occurred, the publishers tender their apologies and invite the copyright holders to contact them.

NovaStar

Text © 2024 Cengage Learning Australia Pty Limited

ISBN 978 0 17 033438 9

Cengage Learning Australia
Level 5, 80 Dorcas Street
Southbank VIC 3006 Australia
Phone: 1300 790 853
Email: aust.nelsonprimary@cengage.com

For learning solutions, visit **cengage.com.au**

Printed in China by 1010 Printing International Ltd
1 2 3 4 5 6 7 28 27 26 25 24

Nelson acknowledges the Traditional Owners and Custodians of the lands of all First Nations Peoples. We pay respect to Elders past and present, and extend that respect to all First Nations Peoples today.

Contents

Changing Movement

Everything in the universe is in constant motion, which means it's always moving. Rain falls from the clouds; birds fly from tree to tree; metal paperclips move towards a magnet. Objects in motion change their position, or move, over a period of time. That movement can be changed by a force, which is a push or a pull on an object. Gravity, friction and magnetism are some forces that can change how quickly an object moves.

A magnet pulls metal paperclips towards it.

Rain falls from a cloud because of gravity.

A bird uses friction between its wings and the air to fly.

Engineers use what is known about forces to design ways for people and objects to move higher and faster, or slow down and stop.

Engineers use their knowledge of forces to design a car.

Three Laws

In the seventeenth century, a scientist called Isaac Newton studied motion and forces. He discovered three natural laws, or rules, about how forces affect movement.

Understanding Forces

Gravity

Gravity is a force that pulls objects towards one another. Objects with greater **mass** attract, or pull, lighter objects towards them. Nothing on Earth has more mass than the planet Earth itself. This means that Earth's gravity attracts everything on the planet towards the ground. Without gravity, objects would float and would never fall down.

A heavy rock stays in place because of gravity.

We use our muscles to fight the pull of gravity and hold ourselves upright. Each time we lift a leg, gravity is pulling it back towards the ground. Whenever an object moves away from the ground, it must **resist** the force of gravity.

Gravity pulls us back down when we jump into the air.

Check Your Height

Gravity is strong enough to make a person become a tiny bit shorter by the end of the day. A person will be slightly taller when they wake up in the morning than at night.

Friction

Friction is a force that slows or stops an object when it touches another object. The longer an object is in contact with another object, the greater the force of friction. It is this force that makes pushing a heavy box across the ground difficult. But if the box is placed on a trolley with wheels, only a small part of each wheel touches the ground. This smaller amount of contact between the ground and the wheel means less friction and makes it easier to move the box.

A heavy object is much easier to move on a trolley, because there is less friction between the box and the ground.

Sometimes it's hard to see friction in action. Air is made up of gases such as **carbon dioxide** and **oxygen**, and these gases are made up of **atoms**. When we move through the air, those tiny atoms make contact with us and create friction.

On a windy day, there is more friction between you and the air.

We can use air friction to slow us down. An open parachute creates friction between the parachute and the air. This slows the fall of a **skydiver**.

Heating Up

Friction between objects makes heat. When you rub your hands together, you can feel the heat made by the friction.

A parachute uses air friction to slow down how fast somebody is falling.

Magnetism

Magnetism is an invisible force that can move objects with either a push or a pull. A magnet is a type of rock or metal. The two ends of a magnet are called its north and south **pole**. When the north and the south poles of two magnets are near one another, they are attracted and pull together. Two north poles or two south poles of magnets push each other away. Magnets can also attract some metals, such as iron.

magnet

Large magnets are used in **recycling centres** to pull metal objects from piles of rubbish so they can be recycled. In **scrap yards**, magnets can be used to lift very heavy things, such as cars. Some special magnets can lift as much as 40 tonnes (around the same weight as a sperm whale).

A large magnet is used to lift big scraps of metal that have been thrown away.

Small magnets can also be used to push and pull small objects. In stop-motion animation films, pieces of metal are often put in the feet of the puppet characters. Magnets placed under the **film set** pull down on the puppets' metal feet, holding them in place so they don't fall over. Under the set, the magnets can be moved anywhere the characters need to be.

Wallace and Gromit are famous stop-motion film characters.

Magnets in Stop Motion

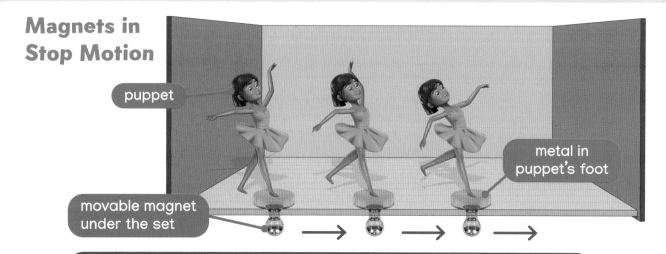

puppet

movable magnet under the set

metal in puppet's foot

The puppet's position and pose are changed slightly for each shot in a stop-motion film. The magnet under the set holds the puppet steady.

Move the Needle

Earth has two poles: the North Pole and the South Pole. Together, these two poles act like a magnet. In a magnetic compass, the tip of the needle is attracted to Earth's North Pole and points in the direction of north.

Forces and Motion
on Land

In Sport

Sports shoe designers think about the different ways friction can affect the performance of the shoe. Usain Bolt, a famous runner from Jamaica, wears shoes with a spiky sole. The spikes provide more contact between the shoe and the ground, which means greater friction, so that Usain's feet don't slip as he runs. This is especially important when he's pushing off at the beginning of a race, helping him to reach his top speed more quickly.

Usain Bolt's running shoes have spikes on the soles.

Usain Bolt pushes off very quickly at the beginning of a race.

World's Fastest Person

In 2009, Usain Bolt ran 100 metres in 9.58 seconds. As of 2023, Usain Bolt is the fastest person in the world.

Basketball shoes have lots of sticky **treads** that create more friction between the shoe and the smooth basketball court. This allows a player to stop quickly to pivot, or turn, and move in a different direction with the ball.

basketball shoes with sticky treads

Basketball shoes help players move and turn quickly without slipping on the smooth court.

13

On a Bike

Rubber tyres, just like the soles of shoes, have different designs depending on how much friction is needed. Tyres on mountain bikes have lots of bumpy ridges to increase friction with the soft ground. This allows riders to keep control and slow down as they ride downhill.

bumpy mountain bike tyre

Mountain bike riders use the bumpy tyres on their bikes to slow down.

Bicycles built for road racing have narrow, smooth tyres to reduce friction with the slightly bumpy surface of the road and help them go faster. In addition, racers wear specially shaped helmets and tight bodysuits to reduce friction with the air.

smooth road racing bike tyre

Road racing bikes need tyres with much less friction than mountain bikes.

François Pervis

In 2013, French cyclist François (say: *Fran-swah*) Pervis set a world record for cycling 1000 metres in 56.303 seconds, or just over 63.9 kilometres per hour (km/h).

On Tracks

Wheel design is just as important when the surface is flat. Train wheels move over smooth tracks built on flat land. The wheels must also be smooth and fit well over the track to prevent unnecessary movement that could create friction.

Train wheels fit into a track.

Some trains are designed to have a front carriage that is pointed, to lessen friction between the air and the train. Many trains can move at speeds of 150 km/h.

A special type of train designed for even higher speeds is called a "bullet train". These trains have even more **streamlined** carriages and very straight, strong tracks. They reach speeds of over 300 km/h.

A bullet train speeds along its track in Japan.

Maglev (magnetic **levitation**) trains remove all the friction between the train and the track by removing the contact between them completely. Strong magnets push the train up and away from the track. Then magnets take turns pushing and pulling, attracting and **repelling** each other to move the train forward. Some maglev trains can travel at 600 km/h.

How a Maglev Train Works

Magnets on the track and train repel each other, making the train levitate.

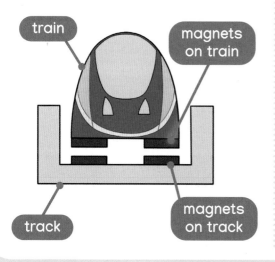

train

magnets on train

magnets on track

track

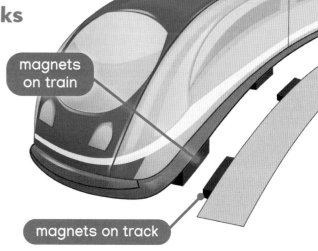

magnets on train

magnets on track

Some track magnets attract the magnets on the train, pulling the train forward. Other track magnets repel them, pushing the train forward.

A maglev train hovers just above its tracks in Las Vegas, USA.

Roller coasters, like trains, also move on tracks. Engineers use gravity to move roller coasters fast enough to travel uphill and around loops. The Kingda Ka roller coaster in New Jersey, USA, is one of the highest in the world. Its top point is 139 metres high. For a short time, riders can experience speeds reaching 206 km/h.

Many roller coasters use magnetic brakes to slow down quickly. Strong magnets are set between the tracks and the wheels, and help pull the roller coaster to a stop.

Kingda Ka roller coaster

Magnetic brakes can be used to slow down a roller coaster on sharp turns.

Other roller coasters, called "launch coasters", use magnets for speed. These coasters use the force of repelling magnets, or magnetic push, to help speed up the ride. With a combination of gravity and magnetic push, launch coasters can reach over 190 km/h in a few seconds.

The Formula Rossa launch coaster in Abu Dhabi, United Arab Emirates, can move riders as fast as 240 km/h.

Formula Rossa launch coaster

Intimidator 305

The Intimidator 305 roller coaster in Virginia, USA, opened in 2010. It was redesigned and slowed down because its high speed was causing some riders to lose **consciousness.**

Forces and Motion in Water

In the Pool

There are many ways to help competitive swimmers move faster in the water. Swimmers smooth out any bumps on their bodies by wearing tight swimsuits and swim caps to cover the hair on their heads. Scientists have discovered that the friction between even tiny hairs and the water can slow down a swimmer. Before a race, many swimmers will also remove all of their body hair.

Tight swimsuits and swim caps mean less friction between a swimmer's body and the water.

Changing how their bodies move in the water can help people swim faster, too. Competitive swimmers twist their hands, arms and legs in certain ways to cut through the water and reduce friction.

Swimmers can use their bodies to reduce friction with the water and swim faster.

David Popovici

In 2022, David Popovici, a 17-year-old Romanian swimmer, swam the 100 metres race in a time of 46.86 seconds, which was a new world record.

On Water Slides

Designers who build water slides use their knowledge of forces to make sure the slides are both thrilling and safe. Adding flowing water makes the smooth surface slippery, and reduces friction between the rider and the slide. Less friction increases speed. If the surface of the slide is bumpy, there is more friction and the slider slows down. Steep sections of water slides use gravity to speed people up, and humps or twists slow them down.

Twists in a water slide help sliders slow down.

Water slide designers try to make new water slides higher and faster. A kind of water slide called an "AquaLoop" drops the rider straight down a long, nearly vertical tube. Gravity speeds up the slider enough to move them up and around a loop. The slider may travel as fast as 60 km/h.

The first part of an AquaLoop slide is so steep it's nearly vertical.

Kilimanjaro

One of the tallest water slides in the world is Kilimanjaro in Brazil. Gravity pulls the slider down to Earth from a height of 49.9 metres, at speeds reaching almost 100 km/h.

Forces and Motion
Through the Air

Planes must resist both the pull of gravity and the push of air friction to reach top speeds. Throwing a paper plane demonstrates these forces. Gravity is always pulling on the paper plane. Once you throw the paper plane, air friction pushes against it as it moves through the air, slowing it down. Once the plane slows down, the force of gravity is strong enough to pull it to the ground.

Gravity and friction both affect the way a paper plane moves as it flies.

Engineers design planes with a smooth, narrow body so they will cut through the air with less friction. Powerful engines keep the plane moving fast enough to overcome the pull of gravity. Passenger planes can fly at 900 km/h.

Gravity pulls on a plane and friction with the air pushes against it.

Speeding Jets

The fastest jets with a pointed, flat design can reach speeds of 3000 km/h.

Forces and Motion Through Space

Astronauts seen floating in the International Space Station (ISS) seem as though they are not affected by gravity. In fact, the force of gravity is still pulling the astronaut and the space station towards Earth. However, the space station is travelling so fast that gravity pulling it downwards makes it travel in a circle around Earth.

Since the ISS is actually always falling towards Earth, the people and objects inside appear to float. This is called **micro-gravity**.

The ISS is always being pulled towards Earth by gravity as it moves.

Many objects on the space station have magnets attached to hold them in place. The astronauts inside the space station must slow themselves as they move through the air or they would bang into things. Many handles and narrow spaces are added to the design so that astronauts can touch or grab them. That friction between the astronauts and the handles and surfaces slows down their movements.

An astronaut uses his hands to slow down as he floats in micro-gravity inside the ISS.

No Air

Outside the space station, there is no air. This means there is no friction. With no friction, objects in space can keep travelling in the same direction forever, without slowing down or stopping.

Designing for Movement

Engineers must use their knowledge of forces to design ways for people and objects to change their motion. Decreasing the force of friction with the ground, air or water helps increase speed, whereas increasing friction slows an object down. Using the push and pull of magnetic force can increase or decrease an object's speed. The force of gravity continually pulls all objects down, so engineers can use gravity in their designs to increase speed.

Knowing how forces work is important when designing faster ways to move and better ways to slow down.

Forces are at work all around us, affecting how everything in the world moves.

Riding a Roller Coaster

by Theo

Last summer, my friend Mason and I were still too short to ride the largest roller coaster at the amusement park. The minimum height was 1.2 metres. This year, we were both finally big enough to take our first ride!

I was nervous as we waited in the long line, but the closer we got to the ride, the more my excitement grew.

I had a huge grin on my face as the bar was lowered over our shoulders and we were strapped into the seat. But as the carriages began to climb uphill, my insides began to quiver. The hill was so steep, it felt like I was glued to the back of the seat. When we stopped, more than 70 metres up, at the top, I took a quick look down. People seemed the size of ants. Then, the carriage we were in gave a small jerk, and I wondered if this was a huge mistake.

Suddenly, we plunged straight down. My stomach fluttered, and I was lifted right out of my seat, pressed against the safety bar holding me in place. I couldn't even catch my breath to scream!

Close to the ground, the tracks took a sharp turn to the right and the speed pushed me hard back into my seat. Before I could think, we were zooming upside down around a loop.

The coaster twisted around corkscrew bends and up and down hills. Just when I thought we were at the bottom, the coaster would rocket back up another hill and drop us down another slope. On some hills I felt like I was flying, shooting into the sky.

When the ride slowed and finally stopped, I discovered I was gripping the bar in front of me so tightly my fingers hurt. I looked at Mason, and he had the same huge smile on his face as I did. It felt like we had flown as fast as superheroes, and at 115 km/h, we were probably pretty close.

After our first ride, there was only one thing to do — line up and go again!

Glossary

atoms (*noun*) — tiny parts that make up all substances

carbon dioxide (*noun*) — a gas that plants take in from the air

consciousness (*noun*) — the state of being awake

engineers (*noun*) — people who design and build new machines or structures

film set (*noun*) — the area with scenery and props where a movie is filmed

levitation (*noun*) — the act of rising and floating in the air without touching anything

mass (*noun*) — how much weight an object has

micro-gravity (*noun*) — a state where objects in space seem weightless

oxygen (*noun*) — a gas that humans take in from the air

pole (*noun*) — the end of a magnet

recycling centres (*noun*) — places where unwanted materials are sorted and reused

repelling (*verb*) — pushing something away

resist (*verb*) — to withstand or fight against something

scrap yards (*noun*) — places where old cars and other broken machines are taken apart so the metal parts can be reused

skydiver (*noun*) — someone who jumps out of a plane wearing a parachute

streamlined (*adjective*) — shaped to move easily through water or air

treads (*noun*) — the ridges on the bottom of a shoe

Index

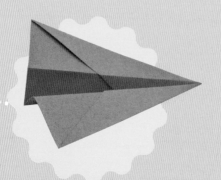